This book belongs to:

Use the stickers at the end of the book to write your name!

Text:
Corinne Delporte

Illustrations:
Annie Sechao

Translation:
Carine Laforest

CRACKBOOM!

T0169833

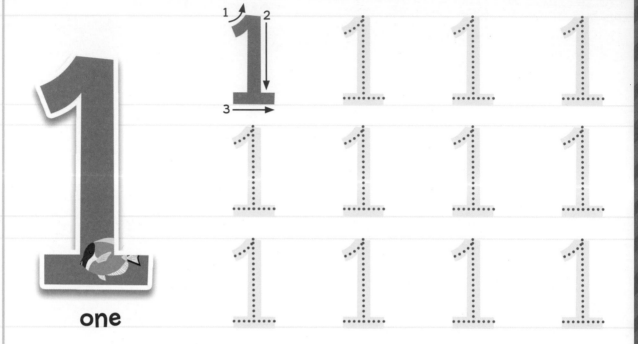

one

two

MATCH THE STICKERS WITH THEIR SHADOWS

There are so many different ways of getting around! Which is your favorite?

school bus

bicycle

airplane

car

train

3

COLOR EACH SECTION OF THE DRAWING THE SAME COLOR AS THE DOTS

COLOR BY DOTS

Venus

IN THE WHITE SPACES BELOW, INDICATE HOW MANY OF EACH OBJECT YOU CAN FIND IN THE IMAGE

Neptune

Mercury

meteorites

Jupiter

Sun

Moon

Earth

Uranus

Saturn

Mars

satellite

The sea is a wonderful place to discover all kinds of creatures.

ADD SOME STICKERS TO THE SCENE

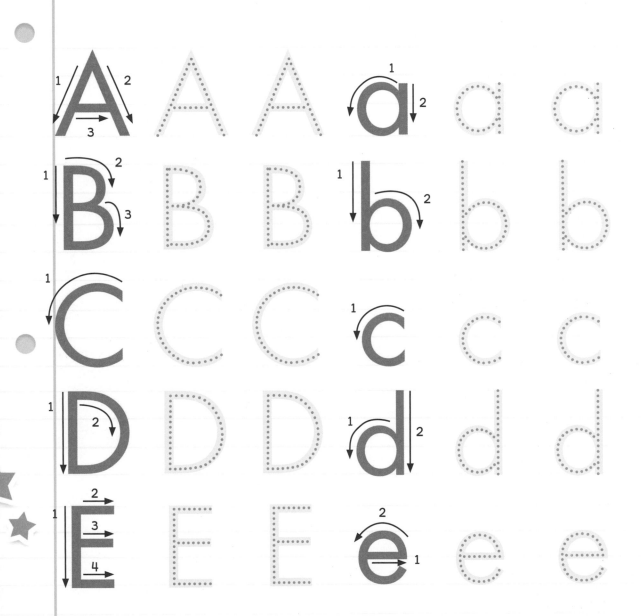

There are so many different birds in the world!

DRAW A LINE FROM EACH BIRD TO ITS SHADOW AND FIND THE MATCHING STICKER

owl

swan

toucan

CIRCLE ALL THE RED ITEMS

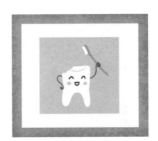

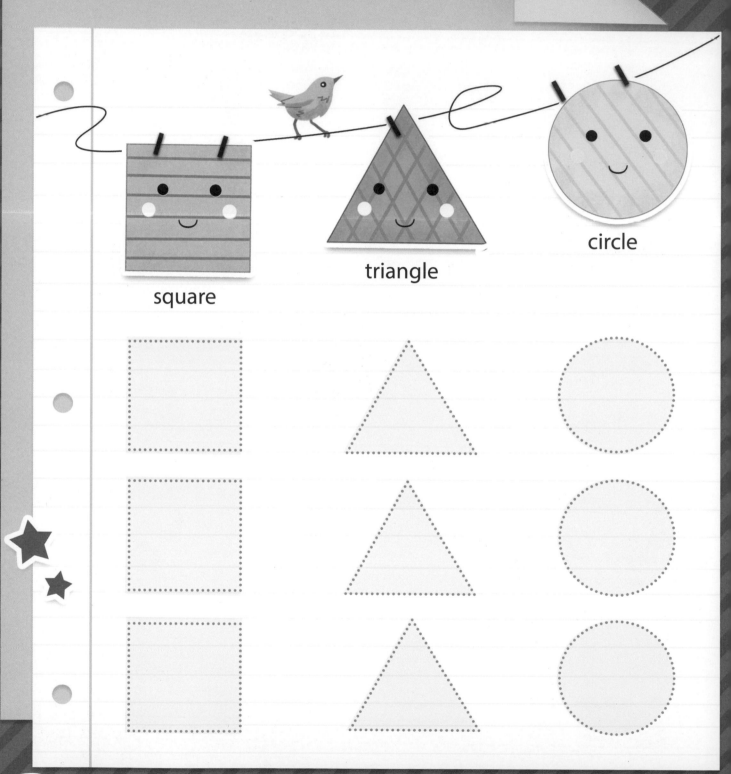

square

triangle

circle

gloves

coat

scarf

shirt

T-shirt

sweater

pants

dress

sneakers

hat

socks

boots

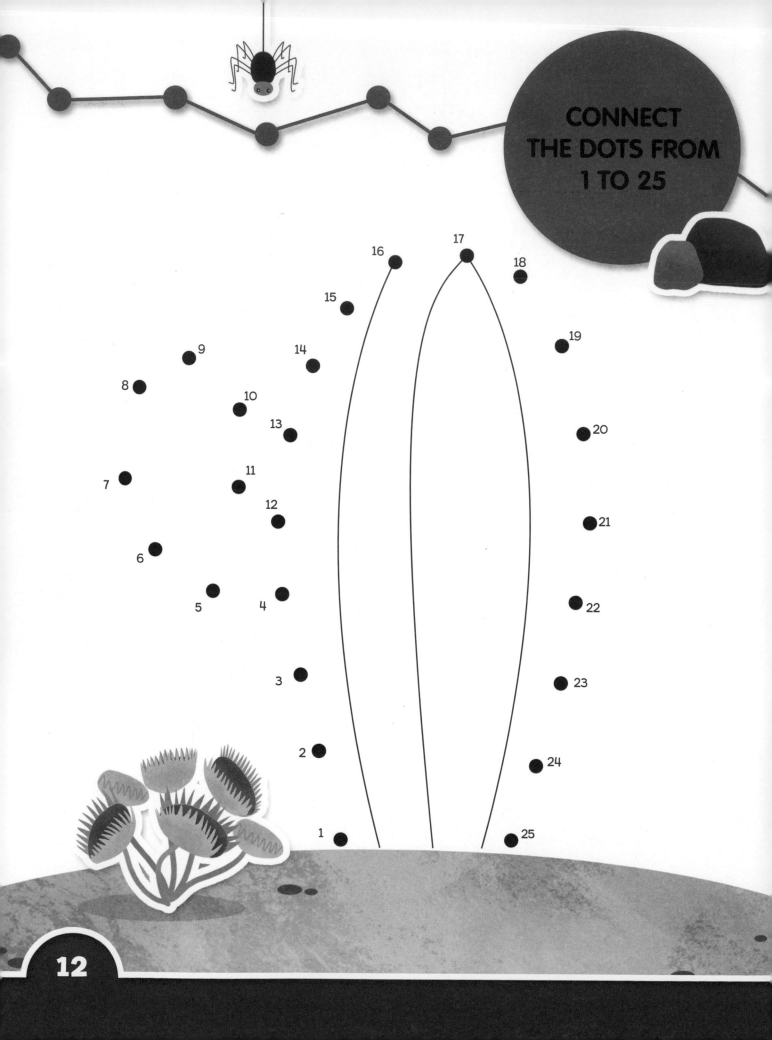

CONNECT THE DOTS FROM 1 TO 25

16

17

18

15

9

14

8

10

19

13

7

11

12

20

6

5

4

21

22

3

23

2

24

1

25

At the market, I saw:
5 apples, **4** carrots, **3** heads of broccoli,
2 bananas and **1** head of lettuce.

FILL IN THE BOXES WITH THE RIGHT STICKERS

14

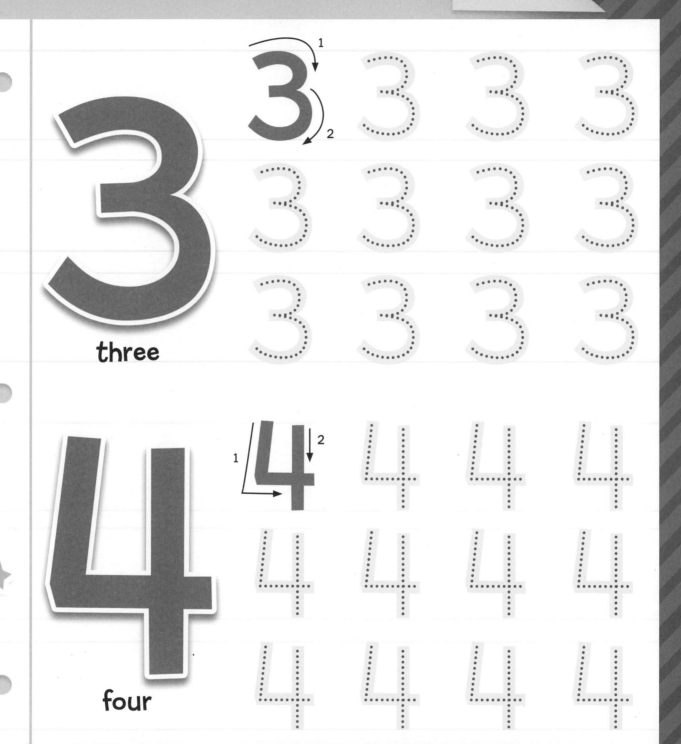

three

four

MATCH THE STICKERS WITH THEIR SHADOWS

Giraffe, horse, rabbit, rooster, cat... Which is your favorite?

horse

cat

rabbit

rooster

giraffe

PLACE THE RIGHT STICKERS ON THE SHADOWS TO COMPLETE THE PATTERN

It's time to play!
What does your room
look like?

ADD SOME
STICKERS
TO THE SCENE

COMPLETE THE IMAGE USING THE RIGHT STICKERS

chimpanzee

chameleon

snake

parrot

peacock

toucan

jaguar

koala

panda

COLOR EACH SECTION OF THE DRAWING THE SAME COLOR AS THE DOTS

COLOR BY DOTS

CIRCLE ALL THE BLUE ITEMS

TRACE EACH SHAPE BY FOLLOWING THE DOTTED LINE

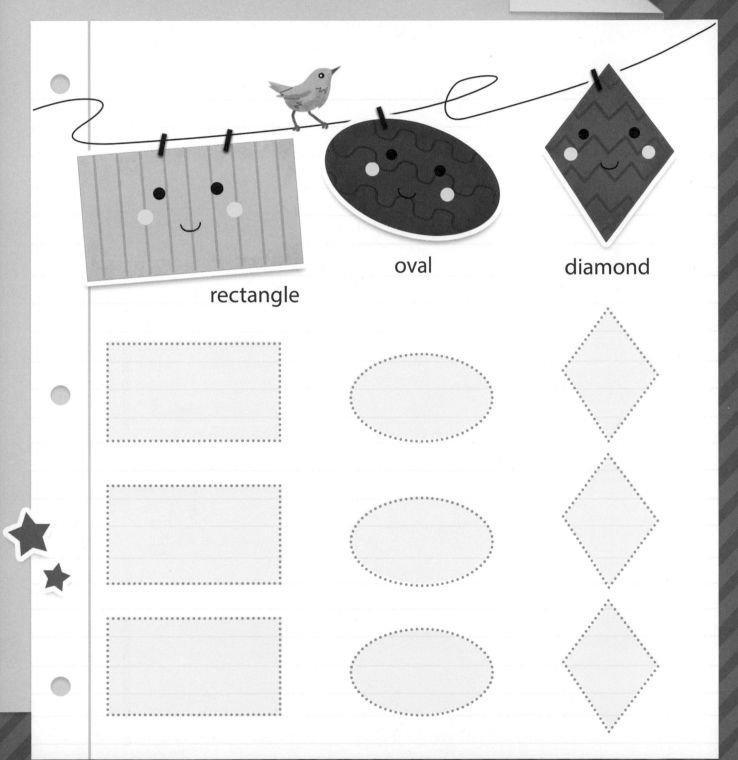

rectangle

oval

diamond

While exploring the cave, I found
5 amethysts, **4** sapphires, **3** rubies,
2 jadestones and **1** amber stone.

FILL IN THE BOXES WITH THE RIGHT STICKERS

Have you ever tasted a tropical fruit?
DRAW A LINE FROM EACH FRUIT TO ITS SHADOW AND FIND THE MATCHING STICKER

star fruit

dragon fruit

durian

5

five

6

six

CONNECT THE DOTS FROM 1 TO 25

HELP THE CHICKS GET BACK TO THEIR COOP

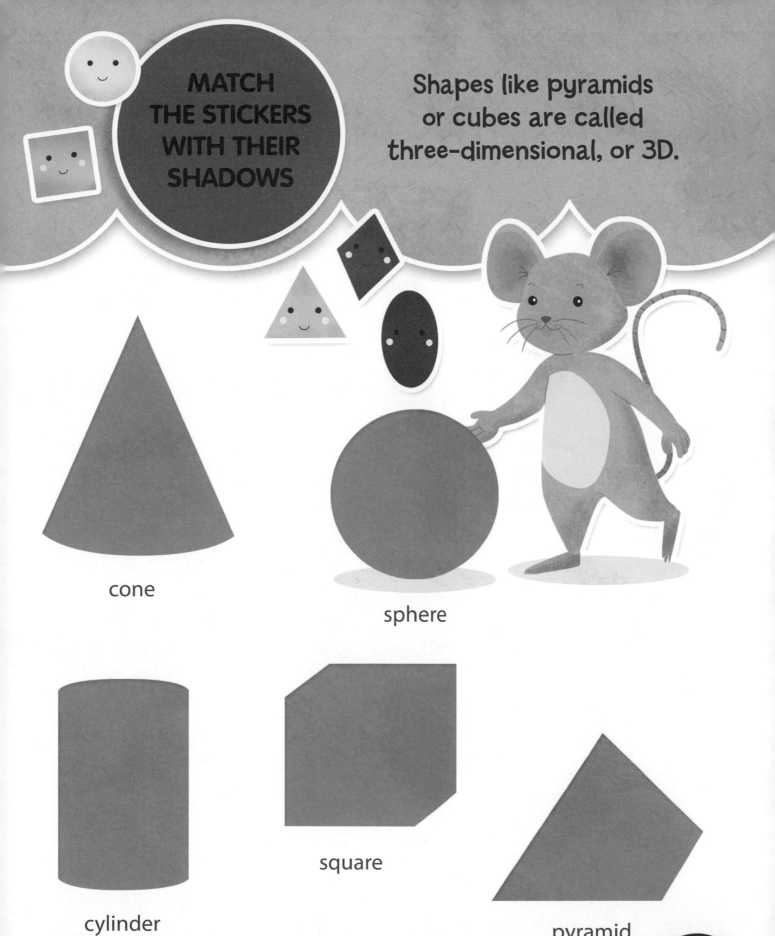

MATCH THE STICKERS WITH THEIR SHADOWS

Shapes like pyramids or cubes are called three-dimensional, or 3D.

cone

sphere

cylinder

square

pyramid

29

squirrel

IN THE WHITE SPACES BELOW,
INDICATE HOW MANY OF EACH
OBJECT YOU CAN FIND IN THE IMAGE

owl

racoon

beaver

mushroom

duck

otter

frog

goose

30

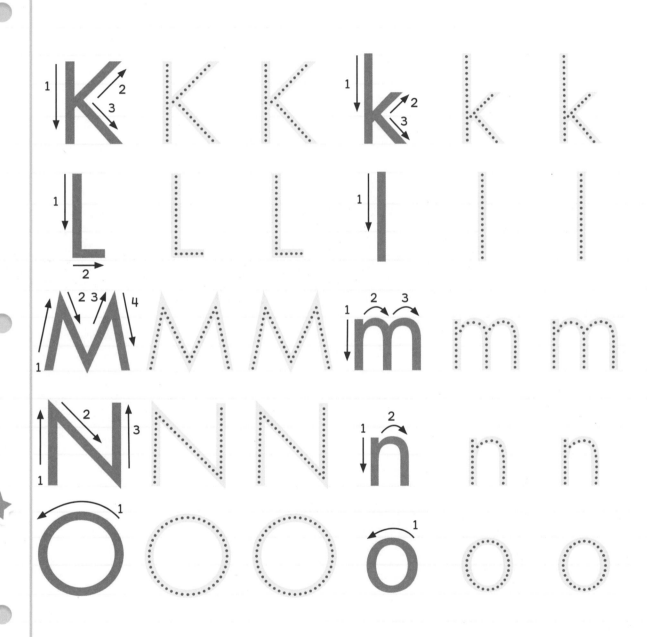

It's very cold in the polar regions, but many animals love it!

ADD SOME STICKERS TO THE SCENE

HELP THE TOYS FIND THEIR WAY
BACK TO THE TOY BOX

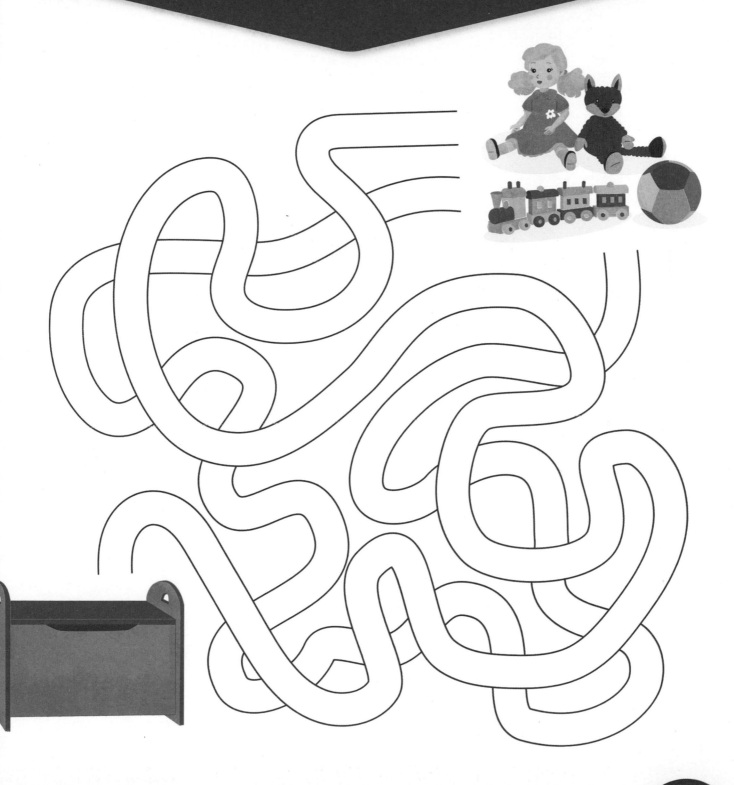

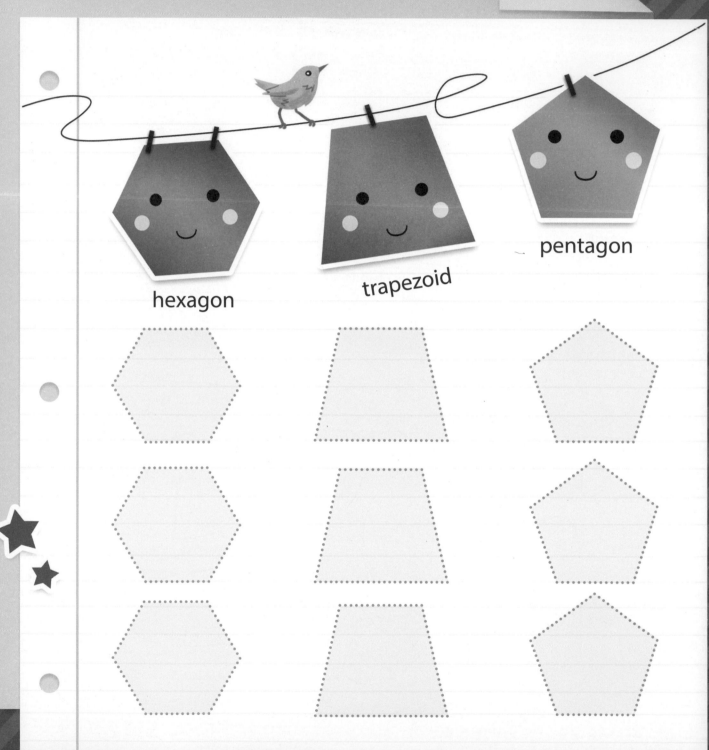

hexagon

trapezoid

pentagon

PLACE THE RIGHT STICKERS ON THE SHADOWS TO COMPLETE THE PATTERN

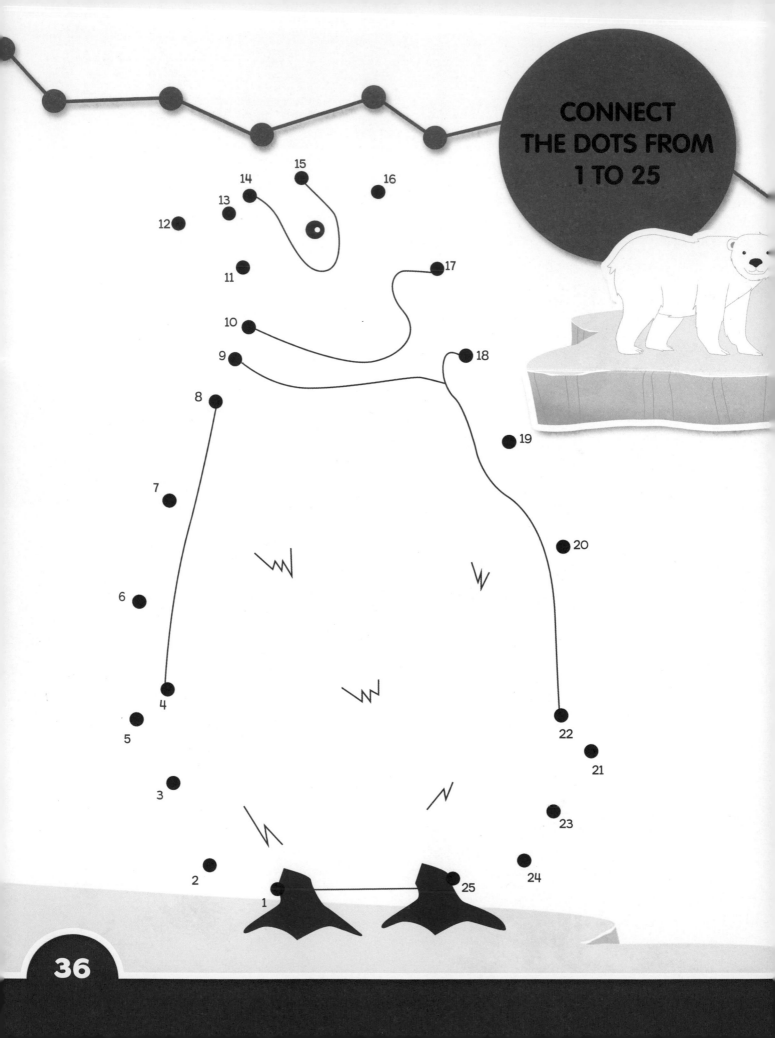

CONNECT THE DOTS FROM 1 TO 25

COMPLETE THE IMAGE USING THE RIGHT STICKERS

whale shark

whale

oarfish

shark

blobfish

anglerfish

manta ray

axolotl

sea horse

MATCH THE STICKERS WITH THEIR SHADOWS

It's lunchtime!
Let's help set the table.

bowls

plates

knife

fork

spoon

glass

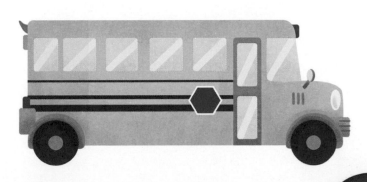

seven

eight

Woo-oo! Make way for the emergency vehicles!

DRAW A LINE FROM EACH VEHICLE TO ITS SHADOW AND FIND THE MATCHING STICKER

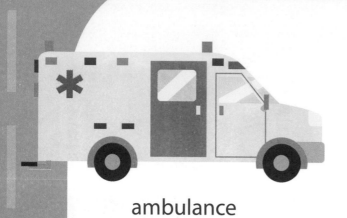

ambulance

police car

fire truck

HELP THE VAN FIND THE ROUTE TO THE CITY

P P P P   p p p p

Q Q Q Q   q q q q

R R R R   r r r r

S S S S   s s s s

T T T T   t t t t

Welcome to the chemistry lab! Are you ready to do some scientific experiments?

ADD SOME STICKERS TO THE SCENE

CIRCLE ALL THE GREEN ITEMS

Music, maestro, please! What is your favorite musical instrument?

xylophone

trumpet

harp

bass drum

violin

PLACE THE RIGHT STICKERS ON THE SHADOWS TO COMPLETE THE PATTERN

TRACE EACH SHAPE BY FOLLOWING THE DOTTED LINE

octagon

star

heart

plant

frame

tooth
brush

soap

toothpaste

bath

towel

sink

CONNECT THE DOTS FROM 1 TO 25

9

nine

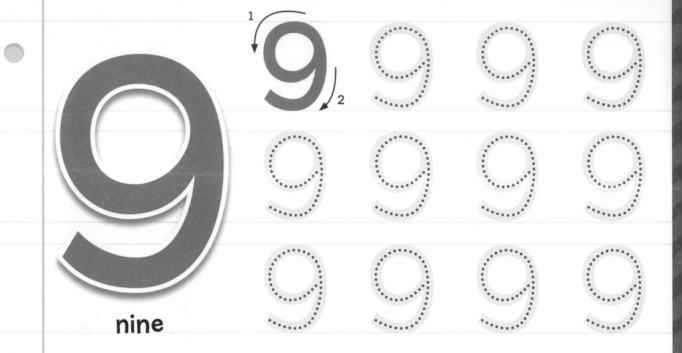

10

ten

In my garden, I saw
5 flies, **4** butterflies, **3** bees,
2 ladybugs and **1** ant.

**FILL IN THE BOXES WITH
THE RIGHT STICKERS**

Animals aren't the only living things in the forest. There are mushrooms too! Have you ever picked one?

ADD SOME STICKERS TO THE SCENE

frame

IN THE WHITE SPACES BELOW, INDICATE HOW MANY OF EACH OBJECT YOU CAN FIND IN THE IMAGE

banner

clock

lamp

plant

sofa

cushion

book

dog

table

HELP THE LITTLE MICE FIND THEIR WAY TO THE ICE-CREAM TRUCK

At the doctor's office, there are many devices that monitor, measure, and weigh patients.

thermometer

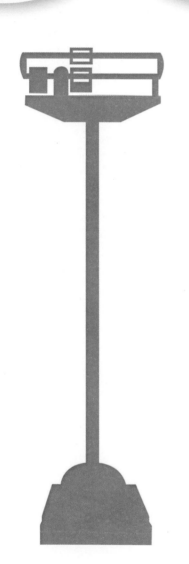

stethoscope

blood pressure monitor

scale

otoscope

COLOR EACH SECTION OF THE DRAWING THE SAME COLOR AS THE DOTS

COLOR BY DOTS

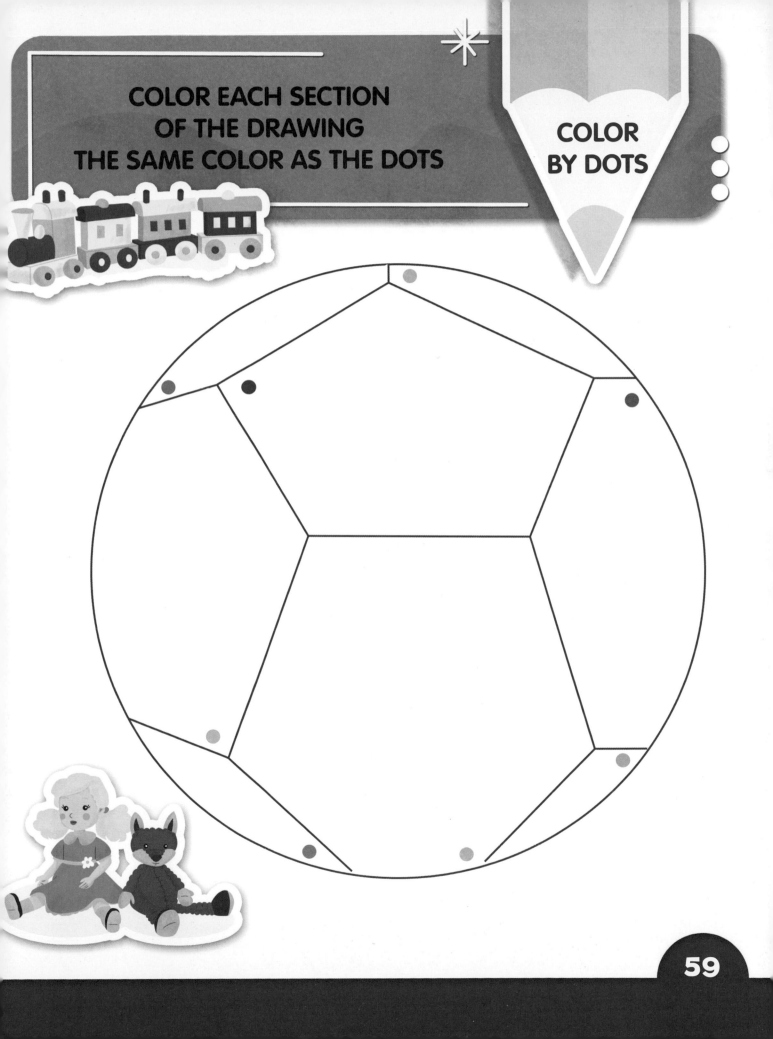

TRACE EACH SHAPE
BY FOLLOWING THE DOTTED LINE

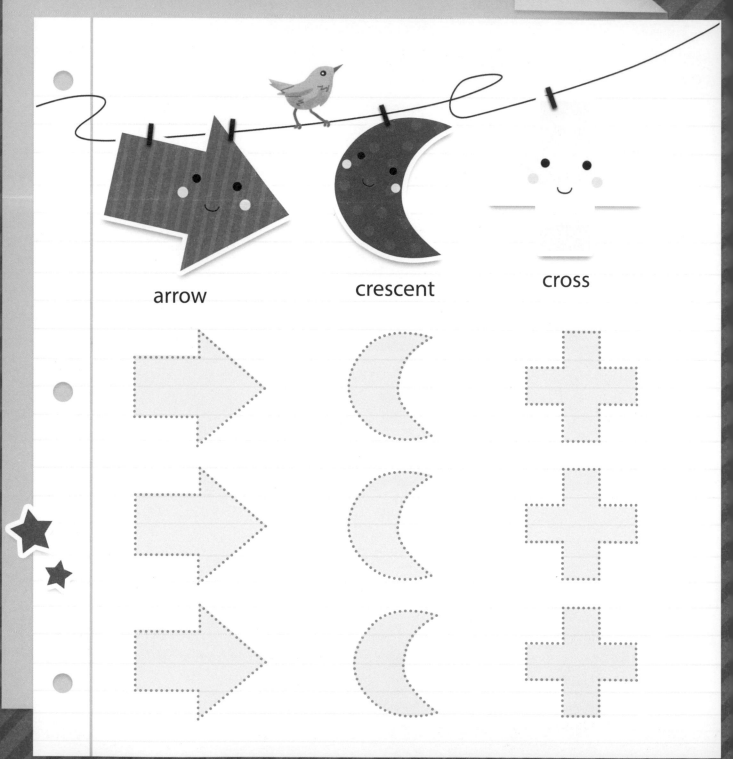

arrow

crescent

cross

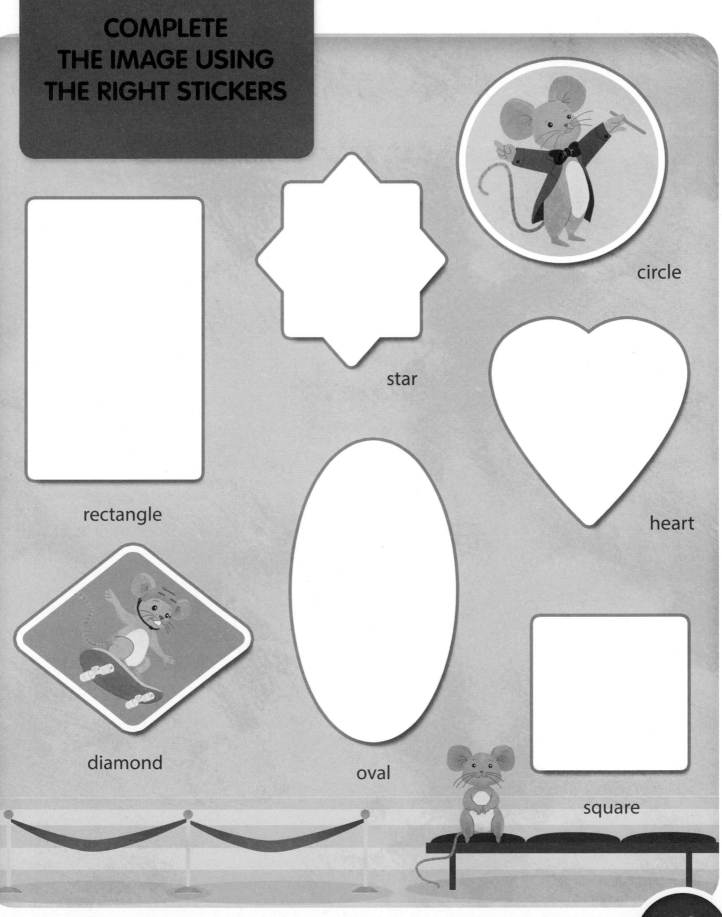

COMPLETE
THE IMAGE USING
THE RIGHT STICKERS

circle

star

rectangle

heart

diamond

oval

square

Speleologists explore caverns and underground caves. Would you like to visit one?

ADD SOME STICKERS TO THE SCENE

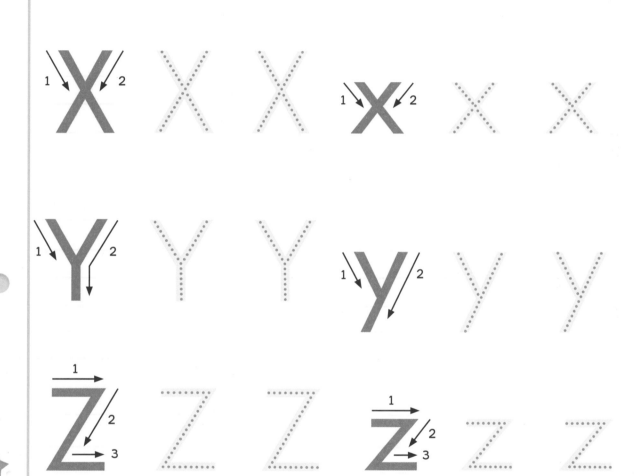

Congratulations!

You made it to the end of your activity book!

You can use the remaining stickers to decorate this page and even write words with the letter stickers!

page 13

page 11

page 16

page 3

page 8

page 6

page 17

page 19

page 20

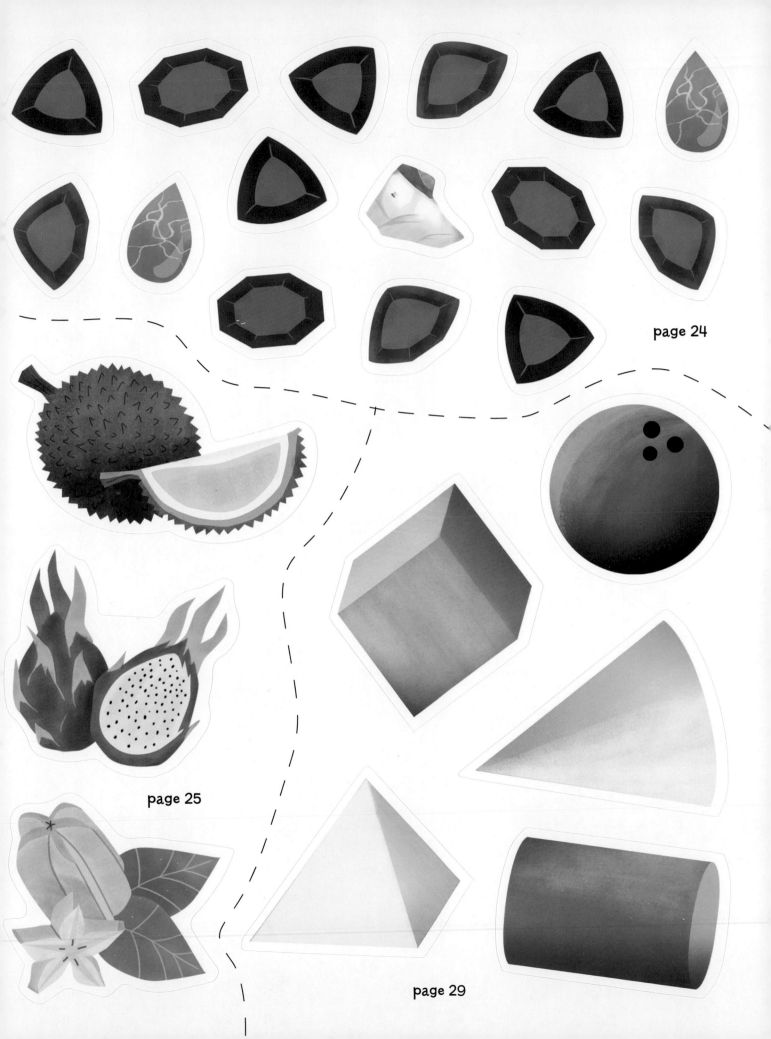

page 24

page 25

page 29

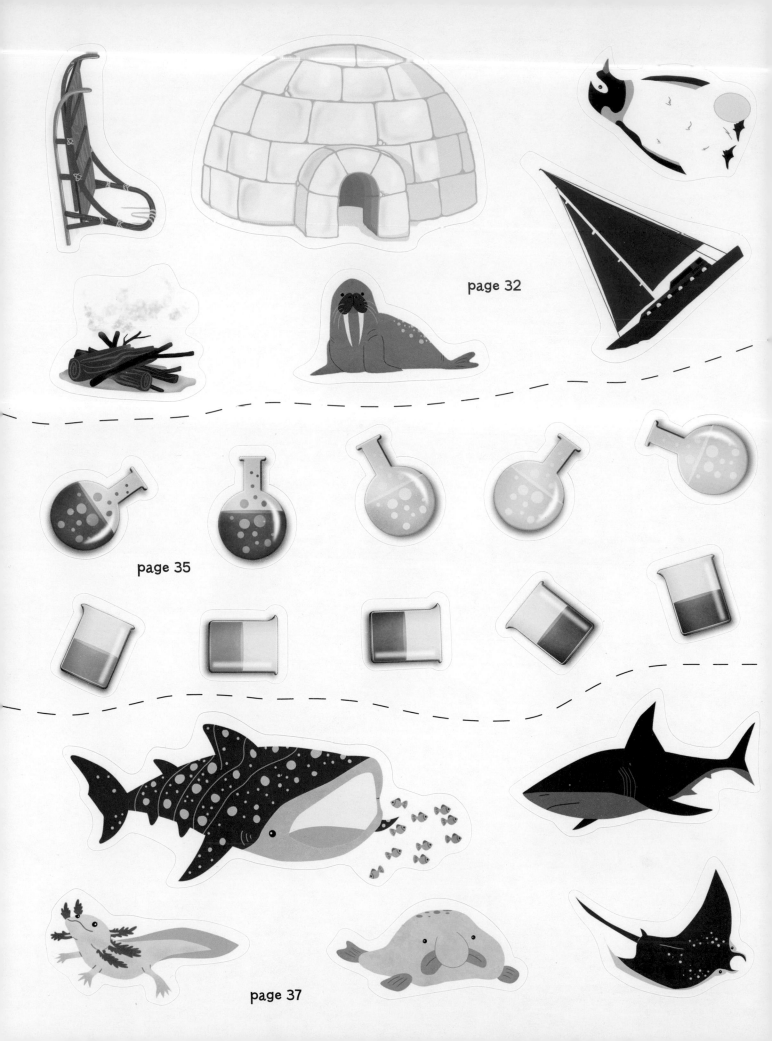

page 32

page 35

page 37

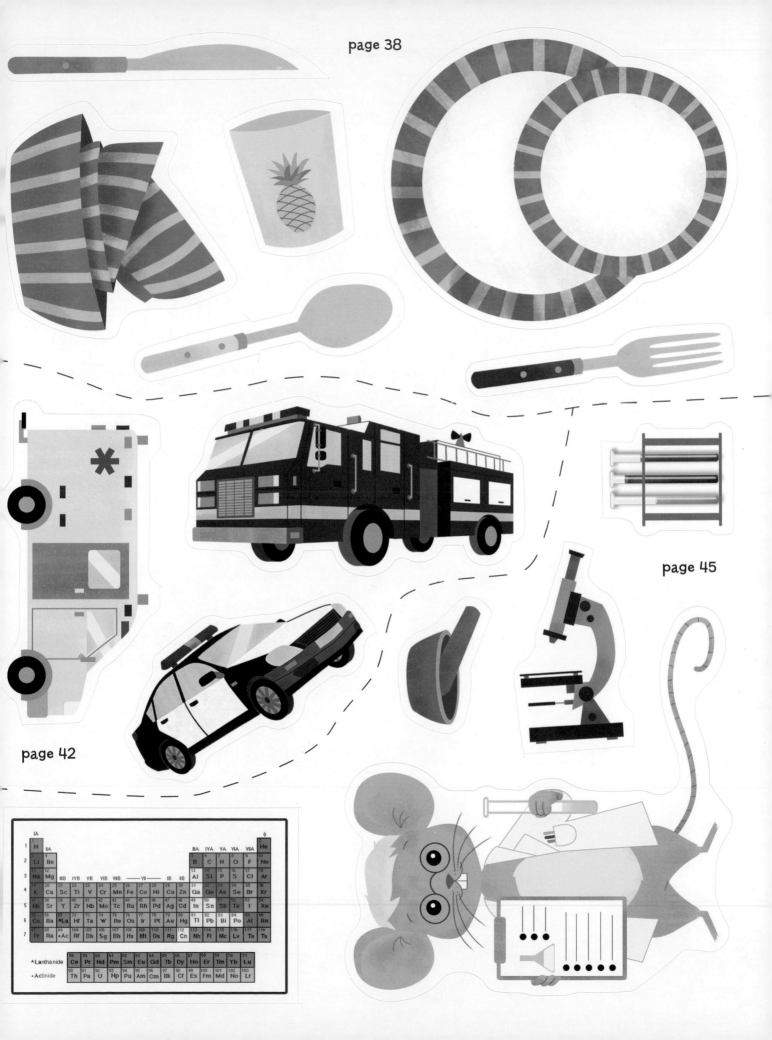

page 38

page 45

page 42

page 47

page 48

page 50

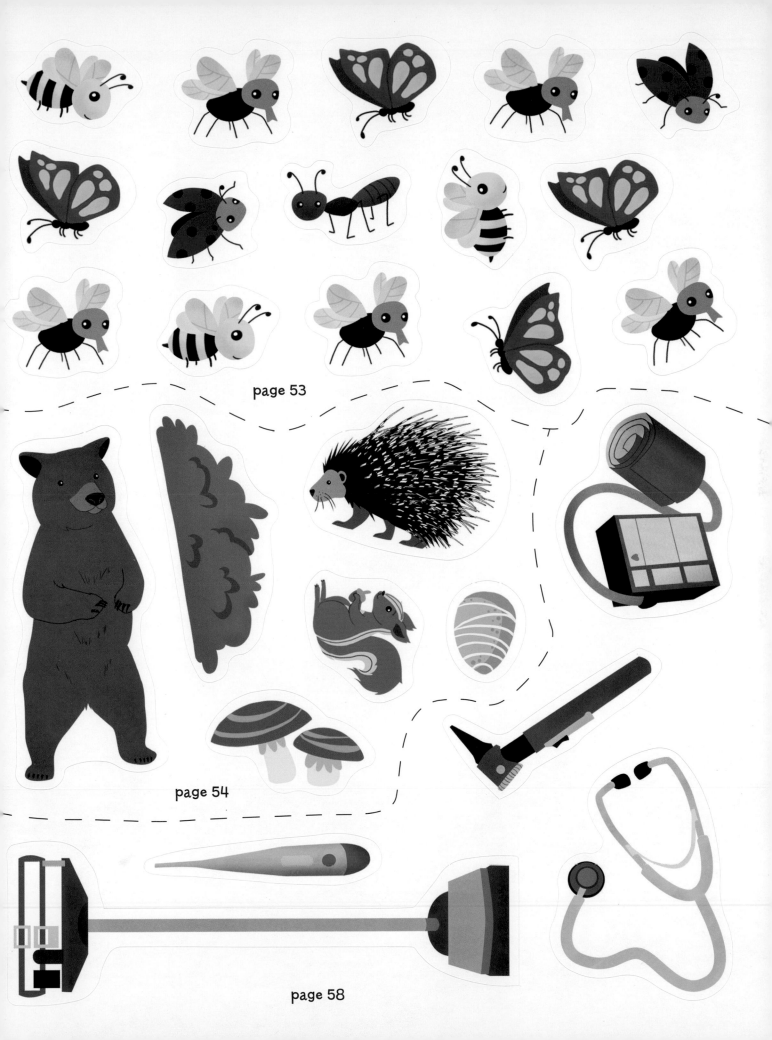

page 53

page 54

page 58

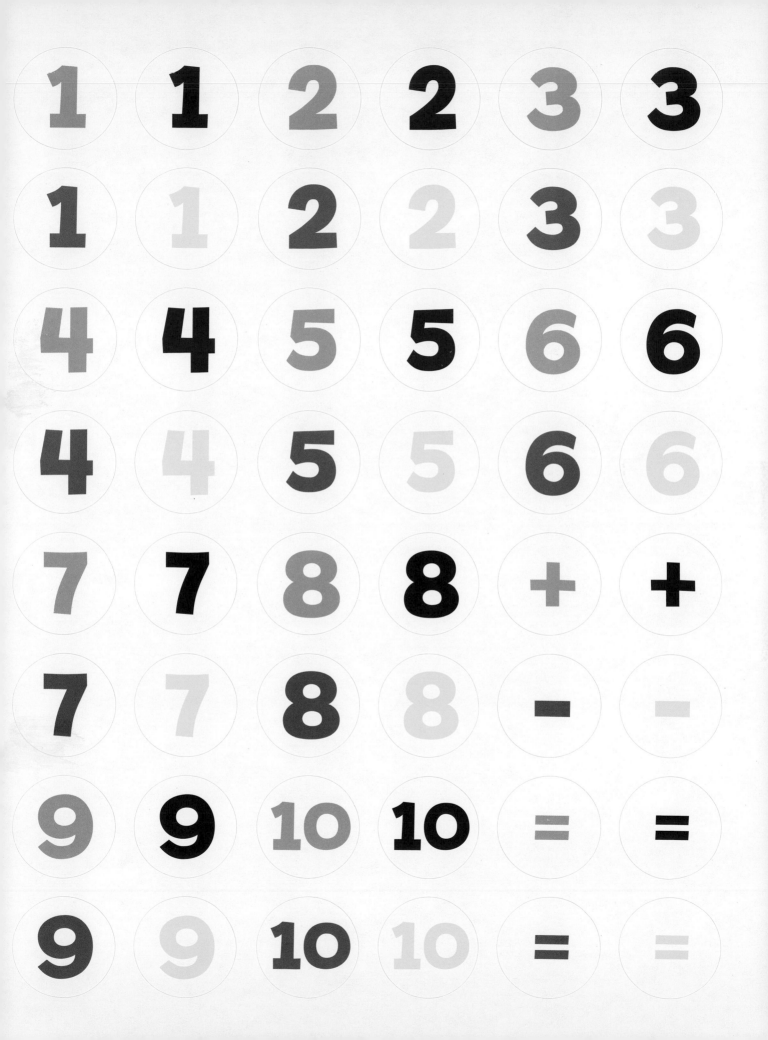

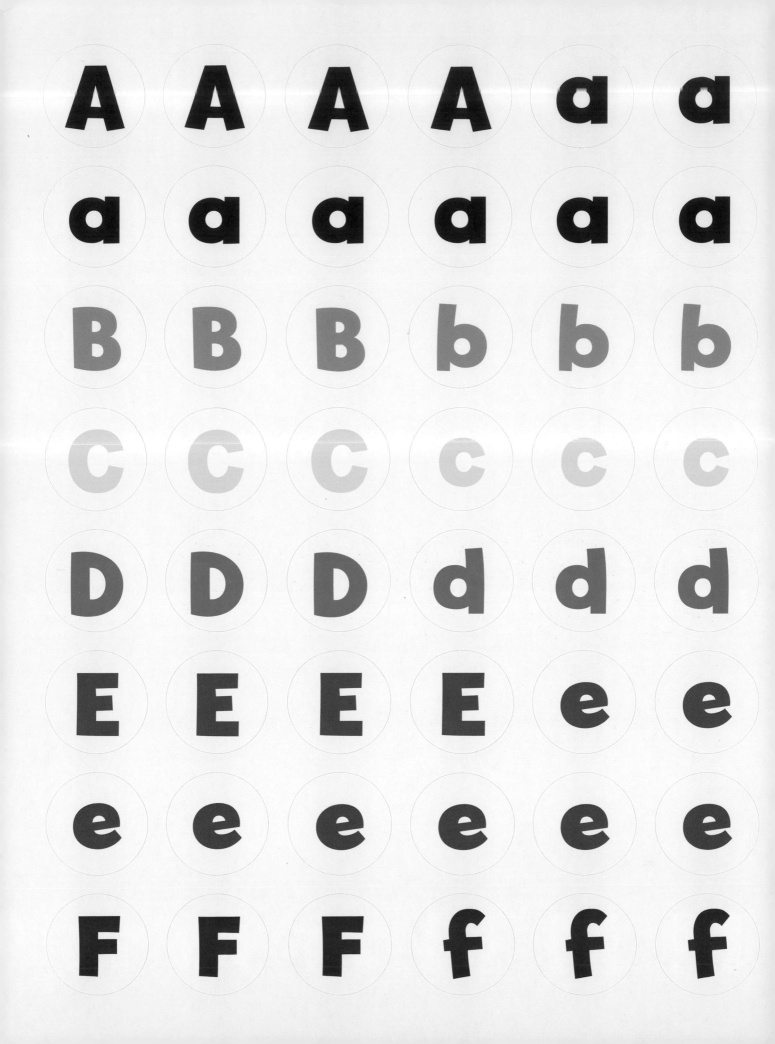

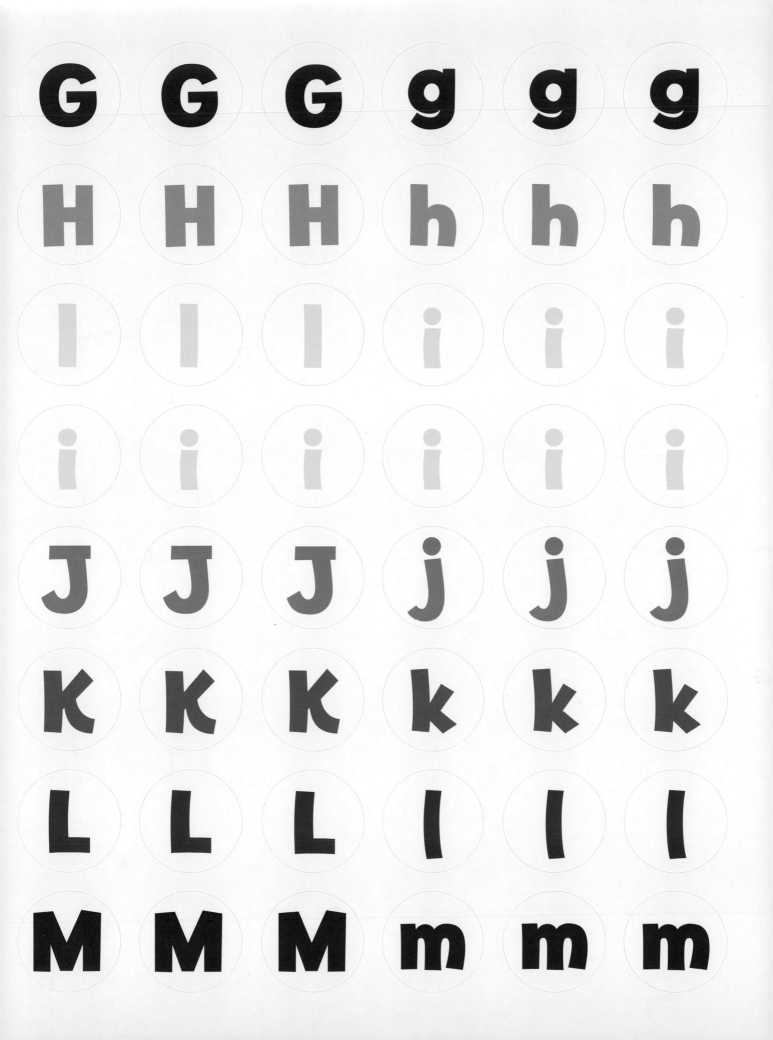

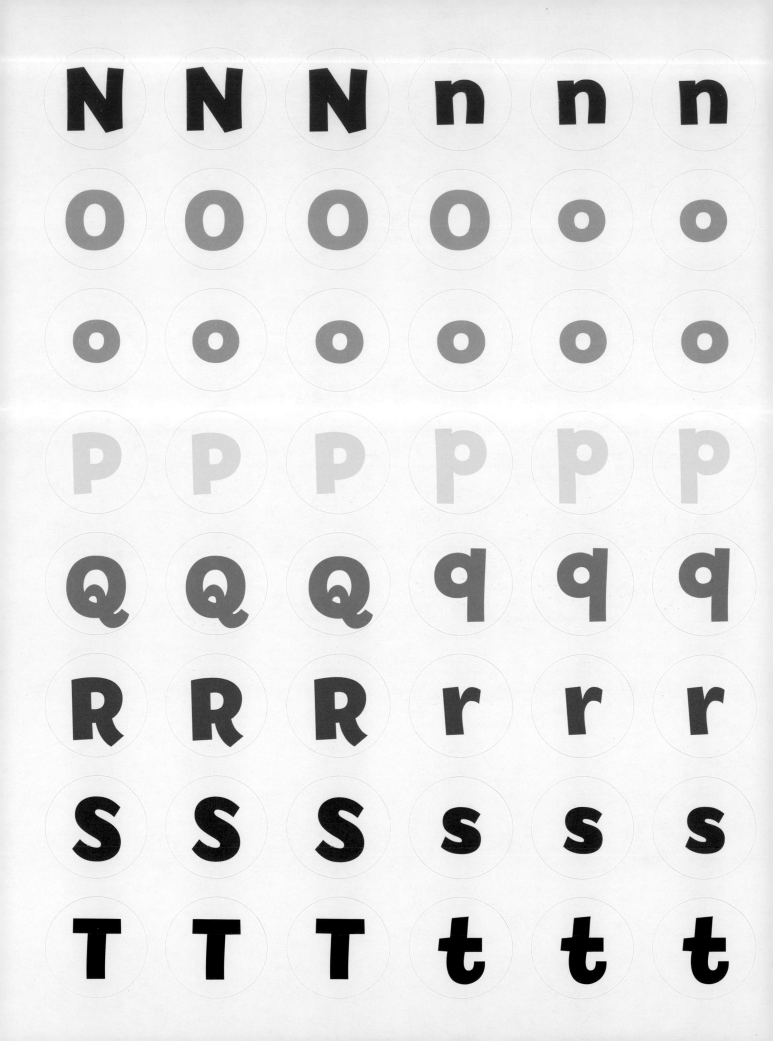

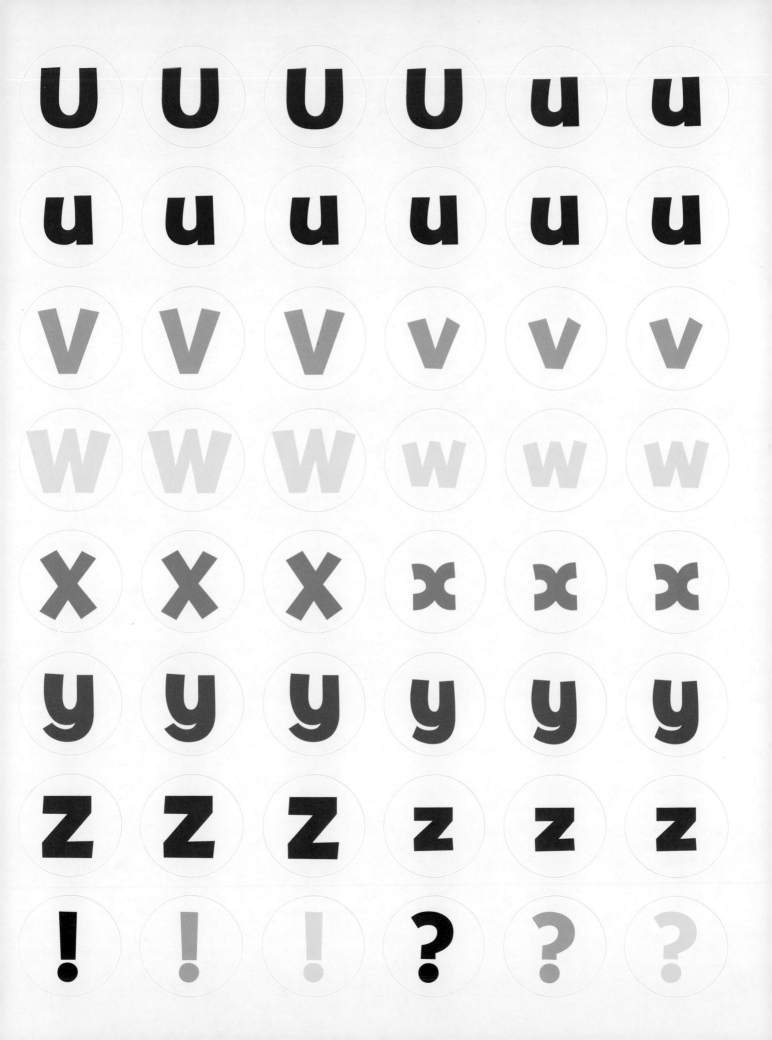